Contents

T0350571

Welcome

1 ✏️ **Match. Then write.**

a. Hello. I'm Rose.

b. _____. I'm Uncle Dan.

c. Hello. _____ Charlie.

d. Hello. I'm _____.

Find and colour. Then write.

1 = red   2 = yellow   3 = purple
4 = blue   5 = pink   6 = green

3 **Find and write.**

yaMdon _Monday_

Fayrid _____

daTsuey _____

taSrayud _____

deWsenyad _____

dunSay _____

hurTdyas _____

  4 **Complete. Then read and say.**

Monday

Tuesday   Hop up and down

Wednesday

Thursday   Stamp your feet

Friday

Say Hurray!

Jump up and down

Clap your hands

5 **Write and circle.** dogs parrots rabbits snakes

Do you like <u>dogs</u>? Yes, I do. / No, I don't.

1

Do you like _____? Yes, I do. / No, I don't.

2

Do you like _____? Yes, I do. / No, I don't.

3

Do you like _____? Yes, I do. / No, I don't.

4

   6 **Read and write.**

Yes, I do.   No, I don't.

1 Do you like parrots? _____

2 Do you like fruit? _____

3 Do you like vegetables? _____

4 Do you like Mondays? _____

7 Find and circle the words.

E	N	M	J	U	N	E	D	L
B	O	A	P	R	I	L	E	J
A	V	Y	L	G	E	O	C	A
U	E	J	U	L	Y	C	E	N
G	M	A	R	C	H	T	M	U
U	B	C	S	J	I	O	B	A
S	E	P	T	E	M	B	E	R
T	R	H	P	B	D	E	R	Y
F	E	B	R	U	A	R	Y	A

8 Follow and write.

1. My birthday is in __October__. I'm _____.

2. My birthday is in _____. I'm _____.

3. My birthday is in _____. I'm _____.

a. **July**

b. **October**

c. **January**

9 **Read and match.**
Then listen and check.

1	What's your name?
2	How old are you?
3	When's your birthday?
4	What's your favourite colour?
5	Do you like dogs?
6	What day is it today?
7	How are you?

a It's in August.

b I'm fine, thank you!

c My name's Rose.

d Blue.

e It's Tuesday.

f I'm eight.

g Yes, I do.

10 **Ask a friend and answer.**

1 What's your name?

2 What day is it today?

3 How are you today?

1 My toys

1 ✏️ Follow and write.

~~ball~~ bike boat car doll kite lorry teddy bear train

a It's a _____.

b It's a _____.

c It's a _____ball_____.

d It's a _____.

e It's a _____.

f It's a _____.

g It's a _____.

h It's a _____.

i It's a _____.

Look. Then read and circle.

1 ((What's) / What are) this?

It's a (ball / (doll) / teddy bear).

2 (What's / What are) that?

It's a (boat / bike / train).

3 (What's / What are) these?

They're (kite / kites / lorries).

4 (What's / What are) those?

They're (bikes / bike / ball).

   Listen and write. Then draw and colour.

1

It's a ___train___.

It's _____.

2

They're _____.

They're _____

_____.

3

It's a _____.

It's _____.

4 📖 ✏️ **Look and match.**

25 — twenty-five

fifty   forty-three

twenty-five   thirty-eight

thirty   forty-six

twenty   thirty-two

fourteen   forty

32   46   50   40   14   38   20   30   43

5 ✏️ **Look and match. Then write.**

1. 20 and 9 is

2. 30 and 4 is

3. 40 and 7 is

4. 30 and 1 is

a. 47 _____

b. 31 _____

c. 34 _____

d. 29 twenty-nine

6 **Look and count. Then write.**

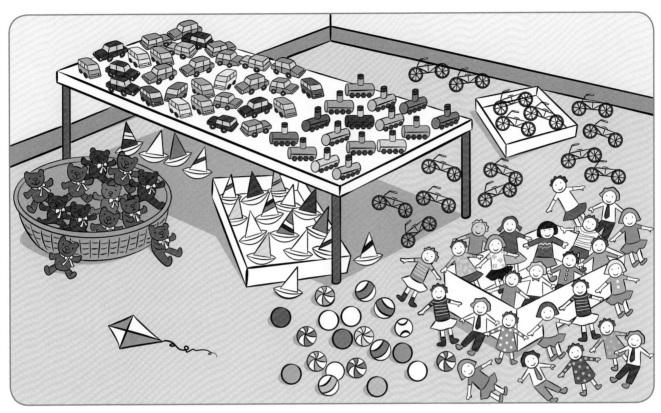

1  How many _____ **bikes** _____ are there?

There are _____ **fifteen bikes** _____ .

2  _____ are there?

There are _____ .

3 _____ are there?

There are _____ .

4  _____ are there?

There is _____ .

7   Look and number. Then tell the story again.

1

8 Look and ✔. Then write about you.

1

2

Good friends play together and share toys.

Good friends listen and help.

Think of a good friend.

_____ is a good friend.

What do you like?

We like _____

and _____ .

9  Read the words and circle.

~~fish~~   rich   shell   ship

10 Listen and link the letters.

ch   c   h   sh

START   p   f   b   **FINISH**

s   sh   ch   s

11 Listen and write the words.

1 ch i n   2 ___ ___ ___

3 ___ ___ ___   4 ___ ___ ___

12 Read aloud. Then listen and check.

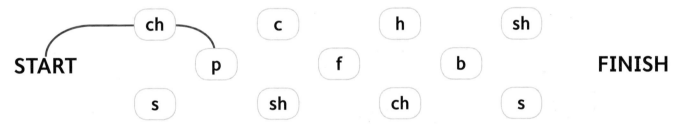

I can see a fish. I can see a shell.

13   **Look and write. Then find and draw the missing word.**

bike   boat   bus   car   ~~helicopter~~   lorry   plane   train

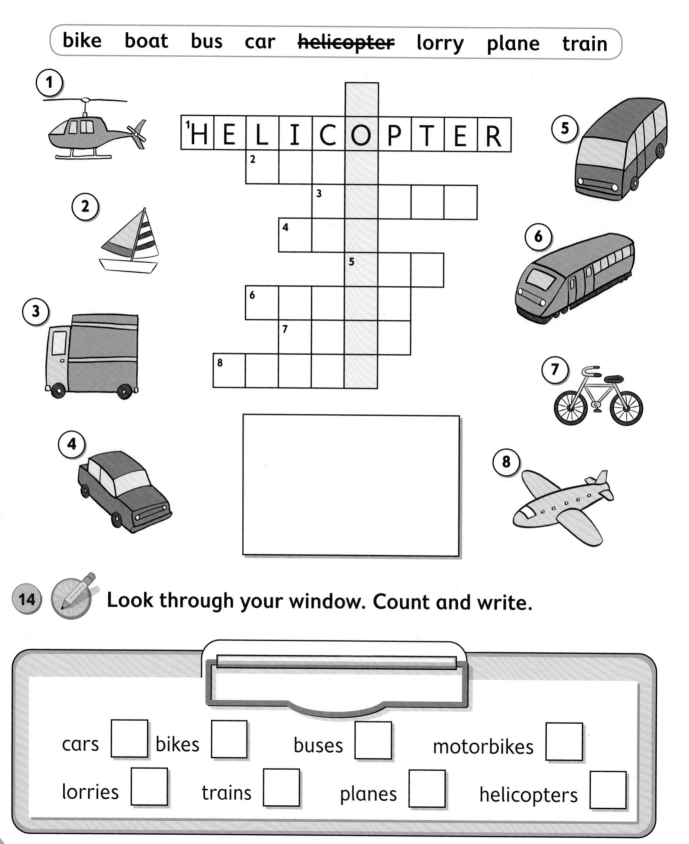

1. ¹H E L I C O P T E R

14 **Look through your window. Count and write.**

cars ☐   bikes ☐   buses ☐   motorbikes ☐

lorries ☐   trains ☐   planes ☐   helicopters ☐

15   **Complete the picture and match.**

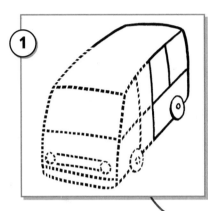

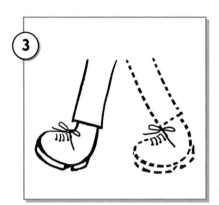

a I walk to school.

b I go to school by bus.

c I go to school by car.

16   **Read and write. How do you travel?**

by bike   by boat   by bus   by car
by helicopter   by lorry   by plane   by train

1 I go to the library _____.

2 I go to the shop _____.

3 I go to the park _____.

4 I go to school _____.

17   **Read and circle. Then colour.**

It's a (car / boat).
It's blue.

It's a (bike / train).
It's yellow.

It's a (doll / teddy bear).
It's purple.

18 **Look and circle. Then write.**

1

(What's this?) / What are those?

It's a _____ boat _____.

2

What's this? / What are these?

They're _____.

3

What's that? / What are these?

_____

4

What's that? / What are those?

_____

19 **Look at Activity 18. Count and write.**

1 How many cars are there? There are _____ cars.

2 How many balls are there? _____

20  **Read and write. Then colour.**

bike ~~favourite~~ school teddy bear

These are my
¹ __favourite__ toys.

This is my favourite
² _____ bear. His
name's Fred and he's brown.

And this is my ³ _____.
It's red and black. I go to
⁴ _____ by bike.

21 **Draw your favourite toys. Then write.**

These are my favourite toys.

_____

_____

_____

_____

_____

2 My family

1 ✏️ **Look and write.**

> aunt ~~cousin~~ daughter
> grandad granny son uncle

This is my dad.

This is my mum.

This is my brother.

1 This is my ___cousin___.

2 This is my _____.

3 This is my _____.

4 This is my _____.

5 This is my _____.

6 This is my _____.

7 This is my _____.

Look, circle and write.

~~aunt~~ cousin daughter son

1 Who's (he / (she))?

(He's / (She's)) my
aunt .

2 Who's (he / she)?

(He's / She's) my
_____.

3 Who's (he / she)?

(He's / She's) my
_____.

4

(He's / She's) my
_____.

 **Look, read and write.**

~~attic~~ bedroom flat hall kitchen living room

Where's my granny?

She's in the ___attic___.

Where's my uncle?

He's in the _____.

Where's my aunt?

_____ in the _____.

Where's my daughter?

_____ in the _____.

Where's my son?

_____ in the _____.

Where's my cousin?

_____ in the _____.

4  **Read and colour.**

1 The red car is on the bed.

3 The blue car is under the chair.

5 The green car is in the backpack.

2 The purple car is behind the backpack.

4 The yellow car is on the desk. It's next to the lamp.

5   **Look at the picture again. Write *True* or *False*.**

1 There are two beds. _____True_____

2 There are three desks. _____

3 There are six cars. _____

4 There's a lamp on the desk. _____

6   **Read and circle. Then match.**

1 Where's Charlie's grandad?
He's in the (flat / (shop)).

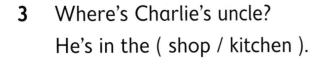

(a)

2 Where's Charlie's mum?
She's in the (garden / bathroom).

(b)

(c)

3 Where's Charlie's uncle?
He's in the (shop / kitchen).

(d)

4 Where's Charlie's aunt?
She's in the (attic / library).

7  **Read and write.**
Then draw your family.

How many aunts have you got?

I've got _____ .

How many uncles have you got?

_____

How many cousins have you got?

_____

8   **Read the words and circle.**

~~bath~~   thick   thin   this

9 **Listen and link the letters.**

| s | th | th | sh |

START   a   r   s   FINISH

th   z   ch   th

10 **Listen and write the words.**

1 th i s   2 __ __ __

3 __ __ __   4 __ __ __

11 **Read aloud. Then listen and check.**

This is a thick book. That is a thin book.

12   **Listen and number. Then write.**

baby   children   grandparents   ~~parents~~

a

☐

_____

b

☐

_____

c

1

parents
_____

d

☐

_____

13 **Read and match.**

1    **2**   **3**    **4**

They're young.   She's young.   They're old.   He's young.

Wider World

14 **Look and write.** | garden   house   treehouse

1

2

3

This is a
_____.

This is a
_____.

This is a
_____.

15 **A treehouse home! Listen and number.**

Read and write. Then match.

1 Where's my daughter?

_____ She's _____ in the garden.

2 Where's your aunt?

_____ in the house.

3 _____ my cousin?

He's in the flat.

  Read and draw.

My teddy bear is in the bathroom.

My ball is on the bed.

My kite is next to the ball.

My doll is under the bed.

 **18** **Read and write.**

aunt garden one these two

This is my uncle and
1 **aunt** and
2 _____ are my cousins.

They are in my 3 _____.

I've got 4 _____
cousins. They are babies.

They're 5 _____
year old.

19   **Draw some of your family. Then write.**

This is my _____
and _____.

_____

_____

_____

_____

3 Move your body

1 **Look and write.**

clap   move   nod   point   ~~shake~~   stamp   touch   wave

Shake your body.   _____ your arms.   _____ your head.

_____ your toes.   _____ your feet.

_____ your fingers.   _____ your hands.   _____ your legs.

2 **Read and circle.**

1

(He / She) can shake
(his / her) body.

2

I (can / can't) touch
(my / your) toes.

3

(He / She) can stamp
(his / her) feet.

4

I (can / can't) wave
(my / your) arms.

3 1:71   **Listen and number.**

a

b

c

d  1

4 **Look and match. Then write the missing letters.**

1

_____ _____ the splits

2

c _____ tch a b _____ ll

3

clim _____

4

thr _____ _____ a b _____ ll

5

stand on your h _____ _____ d

6

swi n g

7

do cartwh _____ _____ ls

8

swi _____

5 **Look, write and circle.**

climb   do cartwheels   ~~do the splits~~   swim

1

Can he ___do the___ ___splits___?

Yes, he can. / No, he can't.

2

Can you _____?

Yes, I can. / No, I can't.

3

Can he _____ _____?

Yes, he can. / No, he can't.

4

Can you _____?

Yes, I can. / No, I can't.

6 Read and match.

1 Jump! Touch your toes!

2 This is fun!

3 Er, can you help? It's the bus.

4 You can push fast!

a

b

c

d

7 Write ✓ = exercise or ✗ = not exercise.

1  ✓

2

3

4

5

6

7

8

(8)  **Read the words and circle.**

ink   ~~ring~~   sing   sink

(9) **Listen and link the letters.**

g   nk   ng   c

START   n   sh   th   FINISH

ng   k   m   nk

(10) **Listen and write the words.**

1 p i ng

2 ___ ___ ___

3 ___ ___ ___

4 ___ ___ ___ ___

(11) **Read aloud. Then listen and check.**

Dad can sing. The girl can sing.

12 **Look and write.**

1

2

hop

3

4

~~hop~~
pull
push
skip

13 **Read and find. Then number.**

	Wave your arms.
	Jump.
	Clap your hands.
	Touch your toes.
	Skip.
1	Hop.

Wider World

14 **Look and match.**

 **1**
 **2**
 **3**
 **4**

a tug of war **b** sack race **c** egg-and-spoon race **d** three-legged race

15   **Read and write about yourself.**

| Yes, I can. No, I can't. |

1 Can you run fast? _____

2 Can you kick a ball? _____

3 Can you touch your toes? _____

4 Can you point your toes? _____

5 Can you throw a ball? _____

16 **Look and write.**

~~climb~~ do the splits hop skip swim swing

1 Can she ___climb___ ?

Yes, she can.

2 Can he _____ ?

_____, he can't.

3 Can he _____ ?

Yes, _____ .

4 Can _____ ?

_____ .

5 _____ ?

_____ .

6 _____ ?

_____ .

17  **What can you do? Read and circle.**

1 I (can / can't) do cartwheels.   **2** I (can / can't) swim.

3 I (can / can't) stand on my head.   **4** I (can / can't) hop.

5 I (can / can't) do the splits.   **6** I (can / can't) run fast.

7 I (can / can't) catch a ball.   **8** I (can / can't) climb trees.

18 **Look and read. Then write *can* or *can't*.**

I ¹_____ **can** _____
shake my body and
I ²_____ skip.
I ³_____ catch a
ball and I ⁴_____
do cartwheels.
I ⁵_____ hop.
And I ⁶_____
touch my toes!

19 **Look and ✓ or ✗. Then write about yourself or a friend.**

I can _____
and I _____.
_____
_____
_____
_____

4 My face

1 ✏️ Look and write.

ears   eyes   ~~face~~   hair   mouth   nose

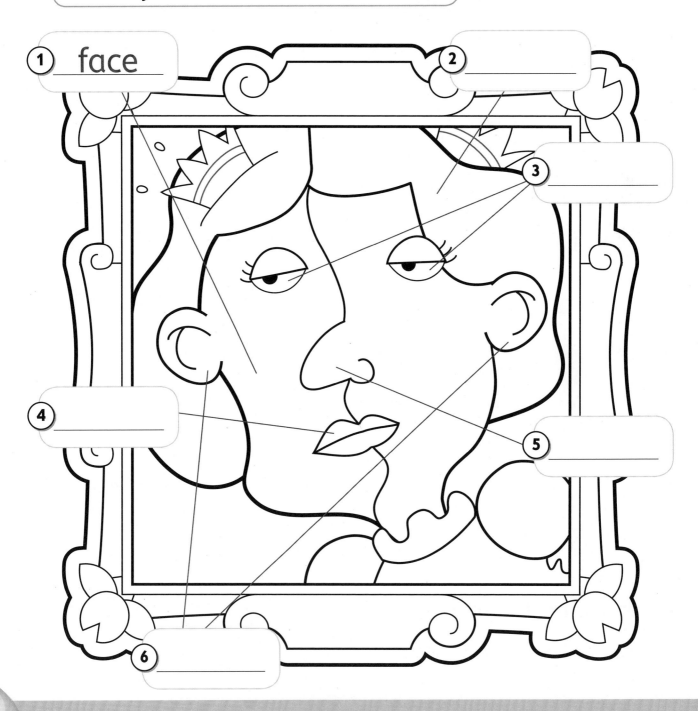

1 ___face___

2 _____

3 _____

4 _____

5 _____

6 _____

2 📖 ✏️ **Read. Then look and write 1 or 2.**

①

②

a) I've got big eyes. `2`

b) I've got short hair. ☐

c) I haven't got a big mouth. ☐

d) I've got long hair. ☐

e) I've got small eyes. ☐

f) I haven't got a big nose. ☐

3 📖 ✏️ **Look, read and circle.**

1 Have you got small ears?

(Yes, I have.) / No, I haven't.

2 Have you got long hair?

Yes, I have. / No, I haven't.

3 Has she got big eyes?

Yes, she has. / No, she hasn't.

4 Has he got a small nose?

Yes, he has. / No, he hasn't.

Read and circle.

1

She's got
(long / short)
hair.

2

She's got
(neat / messy)
hair.

3

He's got
(long / short)
hair.

4

She's got
(neat / messy)
hair.

5

He's got
(blond / dark)
hair.

6

He's got
(straight / curly)
hair.

5 **Listen and ✔. Then draw.**

✔	big eyes		small eyes
	big nose		small nose
	short, curly hair		long, straight hair

6  **Listen and circle. Then look and write.**

| Granny | Ruth | Max | Uncle Ed |

1 (straight) / curly / (messy) / blond   It's _____ Ruth _____.

2 messy / neat / blond / red   It's _____.

3 long / short / straight / curly   It's _____.

4 messy / neat / curly / dark   It's _____.

7 **Look at Activity 6 and write.**

1 Granny has got __short, curly hair_____.

Her hair is __short and curly_____.

2 Ruth has got _____, _____ hair.

Her hair is _____ and _____.

3 Max has got _____, _____ hair.

His hair is _____ and _____.

4 Uncle Ed has got _____, _____ hair.

His hair is _____ and _____.

5 I've got _____, _____ hair.

My hair is _____ and _____.

8 **Look and write.**

1 Has she got a ___small___ nose?

   Yes, she _____ .

2 _____ got black hair.

   He _____ got blond hair.

3 Her _____ is long.

4 _____ hair is messy.

| hair |
| has |
| hasn't |
| He's |
| His |
| ~~small~~ |

9  **Listen and number.**

a

b

c
 **1**

d

10  **Read the words and circle.**

snail   rain   tail   feet

11 🎧 2:19 **Listen and link the letters.**

| ai | e | a | o |

START | ee | ai | ee | FINISH

a | u | i | ai

12 🎧 2:20 ✏️ **Listen and write the words.**

1 s ee

2 ___ ___ ___

3 ___ ___ ___ ___

4 ___ ___ ___ ___

13  **Read aloud. Then listen and check.**

The cat has got a tail. The cat has got four feet.

14 Count and write.

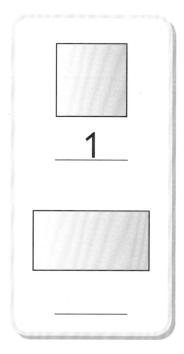

1

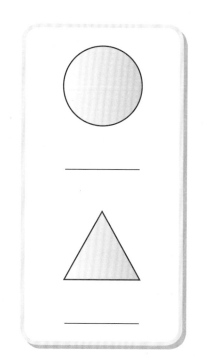

15 Listen, look at Activity 14 and circle.

1 (Yes) / No   **2** Yes / No   **3** Yes / No   **4** Yes / No

16 Draw. Use the shapes in Activity 14. Then write.

It's a _____.

Wider World

17   **Read and circle.**

1

It's a (painting / (mask)).

It's got (big / small) eyes.

2

It's a (mosaic / statue).

It's got (long / short) hair.

18  **Look at the mosaic pictures. Colour and write.**

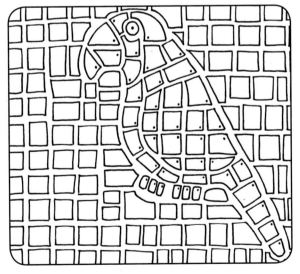

What's this?

What's this?

It's a _____. _____

19   **Read and write.**

1 Has she got big eyes?

Yes, she has   .

2 Has she got dark hair?

_____.

3 Has she got small ears?

_____.

4 Has she got a big nose?

_____.

20   **Draw. Then read and write.**

1 He's got short, blond hair. It's curly. Who is it? It's ___ Nick ___.

2 She's got long, blond hair. It's straight and messy.

Who is it? _____

3 She's got long, blond hair. It's curly and neat.

Who is it? _____

21  **Read and circle.**

me   George

This is me and my best friend. ¹(His / Her) name's George.

My hair is short and ²(dark / blond). I've got ³(big / small) eyes. My eyes are brown. I've got a ⁴(big / small) mouth and ⁵(big / small) ears!

George's hair is ⁶(long / short) and ⁷(dark / blond). His hair is ⁸(neat / messy). He's got ⁹(big / small) eyes and a ¹⁰(big / small) mouth.

22   **Draw yourself and a friend and write.**

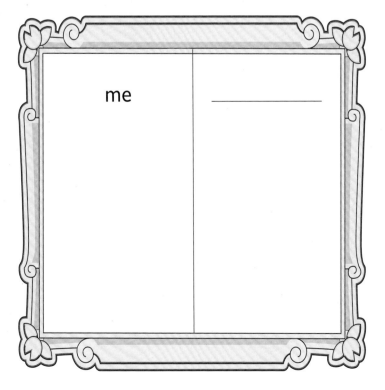

me   _____

This is me and my best friend.

_____

_____

_____

_____

_____

5 Animals

1 Look and write.

cow   duck   ~~goat~~   hen   horse   sheep   turkey

1 goat

2 _____

3 _____

4 _____

5 _____

6 _____

7 _____

2  **Listen and number.**

a  ☐

b  ☐

c  ☐

d  1

3 📖 ✏️ **Look at Activity 2. Read, write and colour.**

1 What are these? They've got big bodies and black feet.
They're white. They've got black faces. They're ___sheep___.

2 What's this? It's got a big mouth and two big feet. It's yellow.
It's a _____.

3 What's this? It's got four legs. It's brown.
It's a _____.

4 What are these? They're big and black. They've got long legs.
They're _____.

4   **Look and write.**

~~bat~~   crow   fox   frog   lizard   owl   rat   skunk

1 ___bat___

2 _____

3 _____

4 _____

5 _____

6 _____

7 _____

8 _____

5  **Read, match and write.**

1 It's got a long tail.
It's brown.

ⓐ  They're _____.

2 They're small and green.
They've got big eyes.

ⓑ  It's a ___fox___.

3 They're thin and black.
They've got two legs.

ⓒ  They're _____.

6 Read and circle the mistakes. Then write.

1

It's a frog. It's (big.)
It isn't __big__. It's __small__.

2

They're goats. They're very thin.
They aren't _____.
They're _____.

3

It's a duck. It's big.

It isn't a _____.
It's a _____.

4

They're skunks. They're green.

They aren't _____.
They're _____ and _____.

7 Look at Activity 6 and write the answers.

Yes, it is.   ~~No, it isn't.~~   Yes, they are.   No, they aren't.

1 Is the hen small?   __No, it isn't.__

2 Are the foxes thin?   _____

3 Is the frog small?   _____

4 Are the skunks red?   _____

8 Read and draw.

What's that?

1 It's a cow.
2 It's a goat.
3 They're hens.
4 It's a skunk.

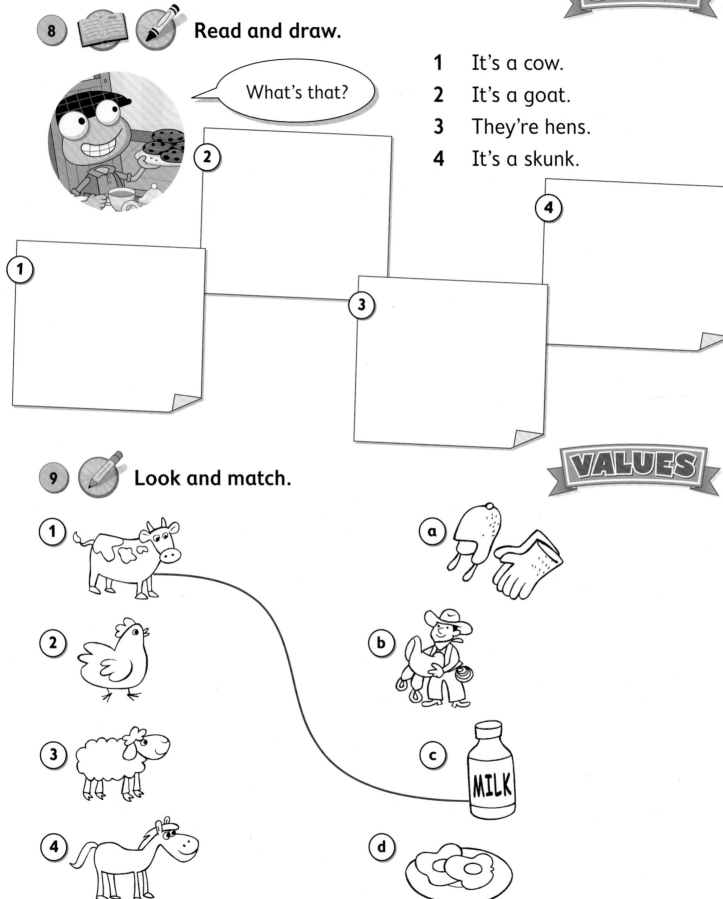

9 Look and match.

VALUES

1
2
3
4

a
b
c MILK
d

PHONICS
igh oa

10   **Read the words and circle.**

~~boat~~   goat   light   soap

11 **2:45 Listen and link the letters.**

a   igh   o   a

START ———— i   oa   **FINISH**

oa   ch   i   igh

12  **2:46 Listen and write the words.**

1 __s__ __igh__   2 ___ ___

3 ___ ___ ___   4 ___ ___ ___

13   **2:47 Read aloud. Then listen and check.**

The goat has got some soap. The goat has got a boat.

14  **Look and read. Then write and circle.**

1

I'm a _____ fox _____.
I'm ((asleep) / awake) in the day.

2

I'm a _____.
I'm (asleep / awake) at night.

3

I'm an _____.
I'm (asleep / awake) at night.

4

I'm a _____.
I'm (asleep / awake) in the day.

5

I'm a _____.
I'm (asleep / awake) in the day.

bat
cow
duck
~~fox~~
owl

15  **Draw the animals from Activity 14.**

1
day

2
night

Wider World

16 **Look and match.**

1  a hen

2  an ostrich

a 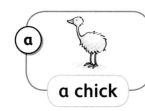 a chick

b 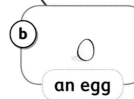 an egg

c 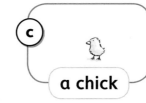 a chick

d 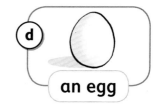 an egg

17  **Read and write *True* or *False*.**

1 Ostriches are birds.   True
2 They aren't big. They're small. _____
3 They've got two legs.   _____
4 They've got very short legs.   _____
5 They can't fly.   _____
6 The father ostrich is brown.   _____
7 Ostrich eggs aren't small. They're big. _____

18   **Correct the false sentences.**

Ostriches are big.

_____

19   Listen, ✔ and colour.

1 **a**  ✔

b 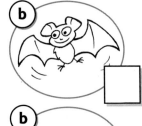 ☐

2 **a**  ☐

b  ☐

3 **a**  ☐

b  ☐

4 **a**  ☐

b ☐

20  Look, read and write.

1 Is the cow big?

_____ Yes, it is. _____

2 Are the sheep white?

_____

3 Is it a hen?

_____

It's an _____.

4 Are they foxes?

_____

They're _____.

  **Read and write.**

| asleep | awake | big | fox | four | horse | tail | ~~white~~ |

My favourite animal is very big and

1_____white_____.

It's got 2_____ legs and a

long 3_____.

It's got a 4_____ nose.

It's 5_____ in the day.

It's 6_____ at night.

Is it a 7_____?

No, it isn't. It's a 8_____!

 Draw your favourite animal. Then circle and write.

My favourite animal is (big / small)

and _____.

It's got _____

_____

_____

_____

_____

6 Food

1 ✏️ 🖍️ **Look and write. Then draw.**

1 eggs ✓

2 _____ ✗

3 _____ ✗

4 _____ ✗

5 _____ ✓

6 _____ ✓

7 _____ ✓

8 _____ ✗

9 _____ ✗

apples
bananas
burgers
chicken
~~eggs~~

fish
pizza
rice
salad

2 **Look and write.**

apples   bananas   ~~chicken~~   eggs

1 I like __chicken__.

2 I don't like _____.

3 She likes _____.

4 He doesn't like _____.

3 **Look at Activity 2. Read and match.**

1   Does Charlie like apples?

2   Does Rose like chicken?

3   Does Ola like bananas?

4   Does Uncle Dan like eggs?

a Yes, she does.

b No, he doesn't.

c Yes, she does.

d No, he doesn't.

4  **Read and answer.**

1   Do you like burgers? _____

2   Do you like salad? _____

5  Look and match.

1
2
3

4
5

grapes	beans
toast	sweetcorn
potatoes	pasta
coconut	pineapple
pancakes	cereal

6
7

8
9
10

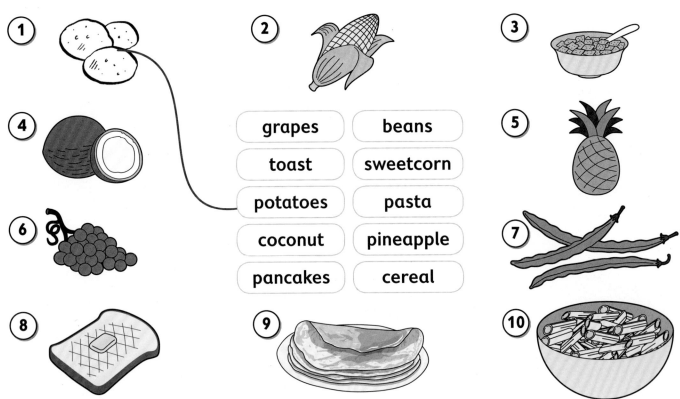

6 Look and write. Then read and number.

~~breakfast~~ dinner lunch

1

breakfast _____

2 _____

3 _____

a I like chicken and apples. ☐

b I like toast and eggs. 1

c I like fish and vegetables. I don't like rice. ☐

7   **Look and write.**

cereal

grapes

fish

beans

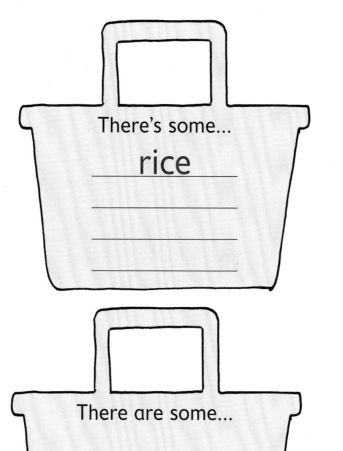
There's some...
_____ rice _____
_____
_____
_____

There are some...
_____
_____
_____
_____

burgers

rice

potatoes

chicken

8   **Look at Activity 7. Read and write the answers.**

~~Yes, there is.~~   No, there isn't.   Yes, there are.   No, there aren't.

1 Is there any rice? _____ Yes, there is. _____

2 Is there any pizza? _____

3 Are there any bananas? _____

4 Are there any burgers? _____

9 📖 ✏️ **Read and ✔.**

		YES	NO
1	Charlie likes apple juice.	✔	
2	Rose doesn't like apples.		
3	Uncle Dan likes pineapple for lunch.		
4	Ola likes banana milkshakes.		
5	Charlie's favourite cake is chocolate cake.		
6	Uncle Dan likes chicken and rice for dinner.		
7	Rose likes milk.		
8	Charlie likes salad for dinner.		

10 ✏️ **Look and circle the healthy food and snacks.**

VALUES

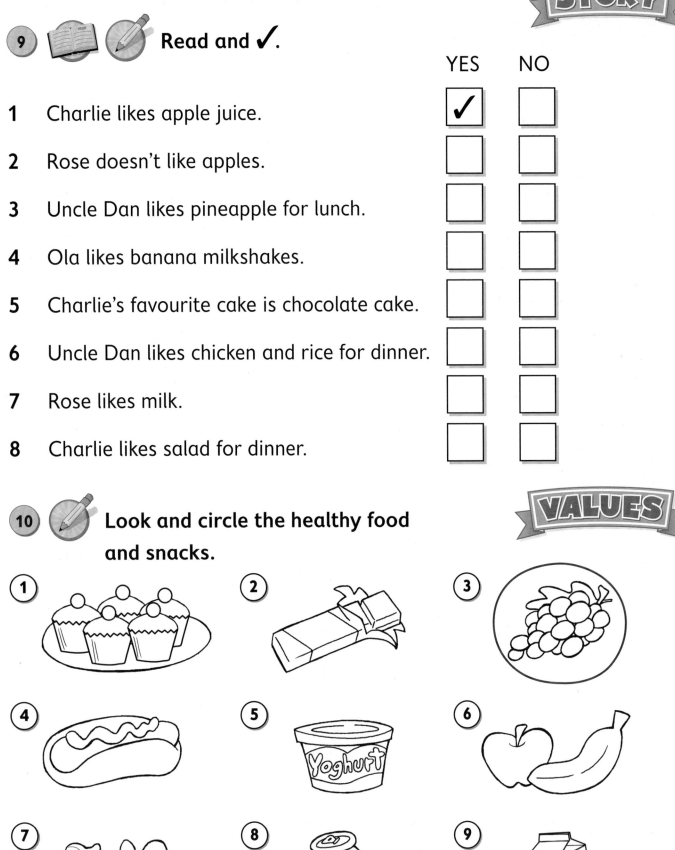

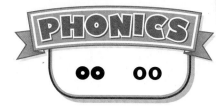

11  **Read the words and circle.**

~~book~~   foot   look   moon

12 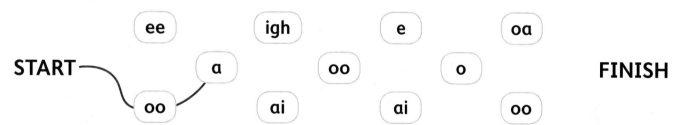 **Listen and link the letters.**

ee   igh   e   oa

START   a   oo   o   FINISH

oo   ai   ai   oo

13 **Listen and write the words.**

1 t oo   2 _____

3 _____   4 _____

14 **Read aloud. Then listen and check.**

Look at the big moon. Look at the book, too.

15   Look and write. | cook   ~~cut~~
fry   mix |

① cut   ② _____   ③ _____   ④ _____

16   Recipes. Read and write.

1

Hot fruit salad

a

Cut some fruit.

b

_____ the fruit in a pan.

c

_____ the _____.

2

Pasta salad

a

_____ some pasta.

b

_____ some sweetcorn.

c

Mix the _____ and _____.

3

Fish and chips

a

_____ some _____.

b

_____ some potatoes.

c

_____ the potatoes.

Wider World

17  **Listen and circle.**

1 She likes (/  / )

for ((breakfast) / lunch / dinner).

2 He likes ( /  /)

for (breakfast / lunch / dinner).

3 He likes (/  / )

for (breakfast / lunch / dinner).

18   **Complete the sentences and write about food in your country.**

	me	my friend
Do you like mushrooms for breakfast?		
Do you like pasta for lunch?		
Do you like fish and chips for dinner?		
Do you like _____?		
Do you like _____?		
Do you like _____?		

19 **Listen and circle. Then write.**

I like...
cereal
chicken
cheese
fish
apples
salad

I don't like...
toast
pizza
bread
bananas
eggs
rice

1 He _____likes chicken_____

and _____.

2 He _____

or _____.

  20 **Read and circle. Then draw.**

This is my breakfast.
There's ((some) / any) cereal and there's (some / any) toast.
There are (some / any) bananas and there's (some / any) juice.
There isn't (some / any) cheese and there aren't (some / any) apples.
I like breakfast!

21 **Read and write.**

any   like   don't   fruit   ~~some~~

This is my favourite dinner.
There's [1] **some** pizza and there's some salad.

I [2]_____ pizza and salad.

There aren't [3]_____ burgers. I [4]_____ like burgers.

And there's some fruit.
I like [5]_____.

But I don't like bananas.

22   **Draw your favourite dinner and write.**

This is my favourite dinner.

_____

_____

_____

_____

_____

_____

7 Clothes

 Find and write. Then colour.

| dress | hat | jacket | skirt | shoe | socks | ~~T-shirt~~ | trousers |

1 an orange ___T-shirt___

2 blue _____

3 a pink _____

4 a red _____

5 a brown _____

6 green _____

7 a purple _____

8 a black _____

2 ✏️✏️ **Read and colour. Then read and write.**

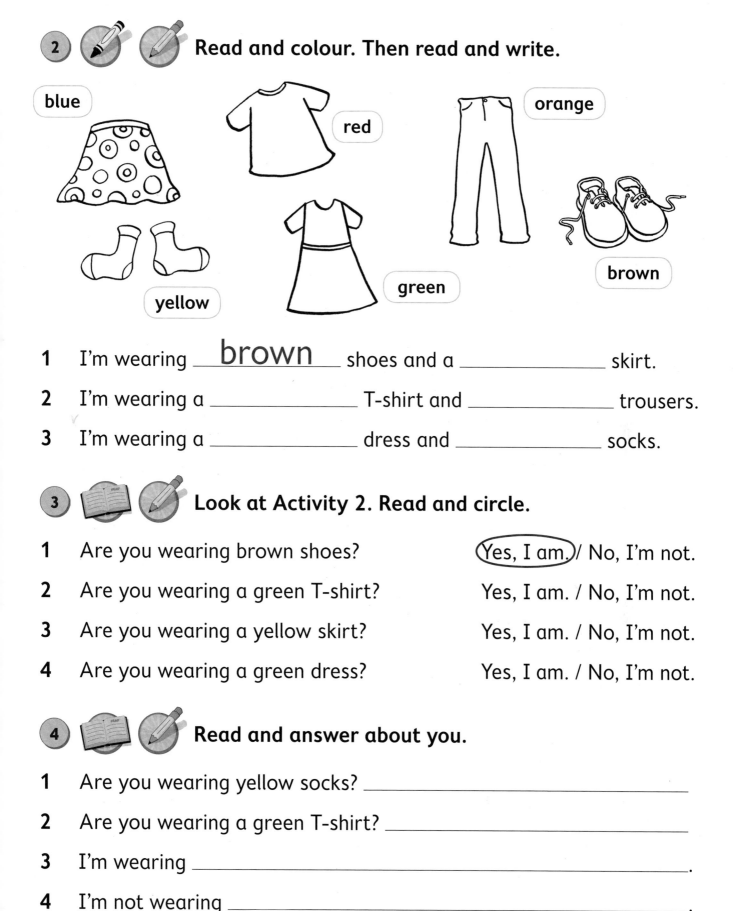

blue

red

orange

yellow

green

brown

1 I'm wearing ___brown___ shoes and a _____ skirt.

2 I'm wearing a _____ T-shirt and _____ trousers.

3 I'm wearing a _____ dress and _____ socks.

3 📖✏️ **Look at Activity 2. Read and circle.**

1 Are you wearing brown shoes?   (Yes, I am.)/ No, I'm not.

2 Are you wearing a green T-shirt?   Yes, I am. / No, I'm not.

3 Are you wearing a yellow skirt?   Yes, I am. / No, I'm not.

4 Are you wearing a green dress?   Yes, I am. / No, I'm not.

4 📖✏️ **Read and answer about you.**

1 Are you wearing yellow socks? _____

2 Are you wearing a green T-shirt? _____

3 I'm wearing _____.

4 I'm not wearing _____.

bed   boots   jumper   ~~pyjamas~~   pyjamas   school   shoes   T-shirt

1 Take off your _pyjamas_ .

2 Put on your _____ .

3 Put on your _____ .

4 It's time for _____ .

5 Take off your _____ .

6 Take off your _____ .

7 Put on your _____ .

8 It's time for _____ .

 **6** **Listen and match. Then colour.**

 **7** **Look, read and circle. Then colour.**

1 Would you like a red jumper?

(Yes, I would.)/ No, I wouldn't.

I'd like a (red jumper / red shirt).

2 Would you like white trainers?

Yes, I would. / No, I wouldn't.

I'd like (a pink boot / pink boots).

3 Would you like a yellow jacket?

Yes, I would. / No, I wouldn't.

I'd like a (yellow shirt / yellow skirt).

4 Would you like blue pyjamas?

Yes, I would. / No, I wouldn't.

I'd like (a blue pyjamas / blue pyjamas).

8   **Colour. Then write.**

1 I'm wearing a

_____

_____ .

2 I'm wearing a

_____

_____ .

9 **Look and write.**

Good morning.   Goodbye!   Good night.
I'm sorry.   Please.   Thank you.

Good morning.

ar ir or ur

10   **Read the words and circle.**

~~car~~ girl shark surf

11  **Listen and link the letters.**

ir — or ur r

START — o ck ir FINISH

ar ai ch ar

12   **Listen and write the words.**

1 s ir

2 ___ ___

3 ___ ___

4 ___ ___

13 **Read aloud. Then listen and check.**

See the girl surf. See the shark surf!

14 Look and write.

chef   firefighter   ~~nurse~~   police officer

1

2

3

4

She's a

nurse .

He's a

_____ .

He's a

_____ .

She's a

_____ .

15 Read. Then look at Activity 14 and number.

a I'm wearing a shirt, a black skirt and black shoes. I'm wearing a hat. ☐

b I'm wearing a white dress, a hat and black shoes. I'm not wearing a helmet. **1**

c I'm wearing a coat and boots. I'm wearing a big helmet. ☐

d I'm wearing a T-shirt and trousers. I'm wearing white shoes and a tall hat. ☐

16   **Colour and play.**

a

b

Are you wearing a yellow shirt?

Yes, I am.

No, I'm not.

17 **Look at Activity 16 and write.**

I'm wearing a _____ shirt and a _____ skirt. I'm wearing _____ boots. And I've got a _____ hat with flowers on it!

I'm wearing _____ trousers and a _____ jacket. I'm wearing _____ shoes. And I've got a _____ hat!

18 🎧 3:26 **Listen and ✓.**

1 purple dress ☐ pink dress ✓ pink skirt ☐

2 black trainers ☐ white trainers ☐ blue shoes ☐

3 purple skirt ☐ purple dress ☐ pink skirt ☐

4 brown shoes ☐ red socks ☐ red shoes ☐

19 📖 ✏️ **Read and number. Then colour.**

1 I'm wearing yellow pyjamas.

2 I'm wearing red shoes.

3 I'm wearing black boots.

4 I'm wearing a purple jumper.

a ☐

b ☐

c 1

d ☐

20 📖 ✏️ **What are you wearing? Read and circle.**

1 Are you wearing pink pyjamas?   Yes, I am. / No, I'm not.

2 Are you wearing white socks?   Yes, I am. / No, I'm not.

3 Are you wearing black shoes?   Yes, I am. / No, I'm not.

4 Are you wearing glasses?   Yes, I am. / No, I'm not.

  **Read and write. Then colour.**

are   is   like   these   this   ~~wearing~~

I'm ¹ __wearing__ my favourite clothes. ² _____ are my favourite jeans and ³ _____ is my favourite T-shirt. My jeans ⁴ _____ blue and my T-shirt ⁵ _____ red. I'm not wearing black trainers. I'm wearing white trainers. I'd ⁶ _____ some black trainers. I'm wearing a green cap.

22 **Draw your favourite clothes and write.**

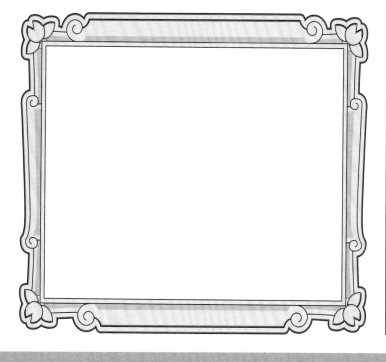

I'm wearing my favourite clothes.

_____

_____

_____

_____

_____

_____

8 Weather

1 Look and write.

cloudy   rainy   snowy   stormy   ~~sunny~~   windy

1 What's the weather like?

It's _____sunny_____.

2

It's _____.

3

It's _____.

4 What's the weather like?

It's _____.

5

It's _____.

6

It's _____.

Listen and write. Then draw.

rainy   ~~snowy~~   sunny   windy

1 He likes __snowy__ days.

2 She doesn't like _____ days.

3 She likes _____ days.

4 He doesn't like _____ days.

   Read, write and circle.

1 What's the weather like today?   It's _____.

2 Do you like sunny days?   Yes, I do. / No, I don't.

3 Do you like cloudy days?   Yes, I do. / No, I don't.

4 Do you like stormy days?   Yes, I do. / No, I don't.

Look and write. ride take fly go ~~make~~ read

1

Let's **make** a snowman.

2

Let's _____ for a walk.

3

Let's _____ a bike.

4

Let's _____ a photo.

5

Let's _____ a kite.

6

Let's _____ a book.

   Look, read and write.

Monday	Tuesday	Wednesday	Thursday	Friday	Saturday

1 It's snowy. What day is it today? It's __**Saturday**__.

2 It's windy. What day is it today? It's _____.

3 It's rainy. What day is it today? It's _____.

4 It's sunny. What day is it today? It's _____.

5 It's stormy. What day is it today? It's _____.

6 It's cloudy. What day is it today? It's _____.

6 **Look and circle.**

1

That hat is (mine / yours)!

2

This hat is (mine / yours)!

3

Those boots are (mine / yours)!

4

And these boots are (mine / yours)!

7 **Follow and write _his_ or _hers_.**

a — These shoes are _hers_.

b — These trainers are _____.

c — This kite is _____.

d — This bike is _____.

8 **Look and number. Then write.**

It's _____.

It's __ rainy __.

1

It's _____.

It's _____.

9 **Look and ✓ the things you can share with other people.**

	friend(s)	sister(s)	brother(s)	parents

(10)   **Read the words and circle.**

~~boy~~ cow cowboy down

(11)  **Listen and link the letters.**

ar   o   h   w

START   j   oy   oy   FINISH

ow — y   p   ow

(12) **Listen and write the words.**

1 __ow l__   2 _____

3 _____   4 _____

(13) **Read aloud. Then listen and check.**

The boy watches the cowboy. The cow watches the boy.

14   **Look and write. Then listen and number.**

~~cold~~   freezing   hot   warm

a

b

c

d

1

cold

---

15  **Read, look and ✓ or ✗.**

Monday	Tuesday	Wednesday	Thursday	Friday	Saturday	Sunday

1 It's Tuesday. It's windy.   ✓   **2** It's Saturday. It's stormy.   ☐

3 It's Thursday. It's rainy.   ☐   **4** It's Sunday. It's cloudy.   ☐

5 It's Monday. It's snowy.   ☐   **6** It's Friday. It's sunny.   ☐

Wider World

16 3:49   **Listen and write.**

~~August~~ January July March September

1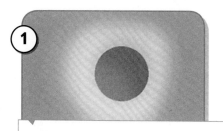

It's ___August___.
It's ___summer___. It's sunny.

2

It's _____.
It's _____. It's windy.

3

It's _____.
_____
_____ snowy.

4

_____
_____
_____

17  **What's your favourite weather? Read and write.**

My birthday is in _____.

The weather is _____.

My favourite month is _____.

The weather is _____.

Picture A

Picture B

1 It's cloudy. **A**

2 I'm wearing a T-shirt and trousers.

3 I've got a train.

4 I like pizza.

5 I'm wearing a dress.

6 I've got a doll.

7 I like chicken.

8 Look at my dog. It's big.

9 It's sunny.

10 I'm wearing boots.

19  **Read and write.**

ABOUT ME

boots   cold   ~~December~~   doesn't   hat   snowman

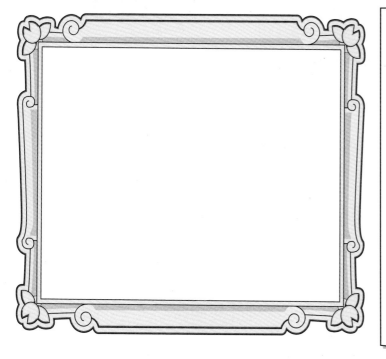

My favourite month is
<u>¹ December</u>.
It's ² _____ and snowy
in my country. I'm wearing a
coat and big ³ _____.
This ⁴ _____ is
mine. He's got a ⁵ _____!
My cat ⁶ _____ like
the snow.

20   **Draw your favourite month and write.**

My favourite month is

_____.

_____

_____

_____

_____

_____

Goodbye

1 Look and write.

~~castle~~　cave　clothes　dinner　doctor
farmer　mountain　shopping

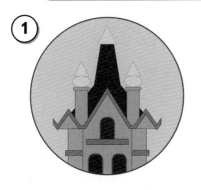　(1)

　(2)

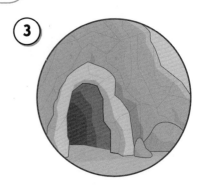　(3)

castle　_____　_____

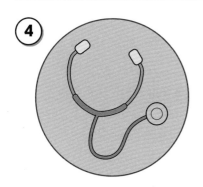　(4)

　(5)

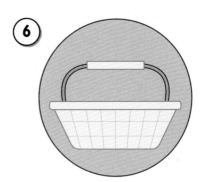　(6)

_____　_____　_____

　(7)

　(8)

_____

2 **Read and draw.**

1 There's a photo on the TV.   **2** There is a key in the door.

3 There are some shoes under the sofa.   **4** There's a duck in the box.

5 There are some sunglasses next to the lamp.   **6** There's an umbrella behind the bag.

  3 **Look at Activity 2. Read, circle and write.**

1 Where (is / **are**) the shoes?   It's / **They're** <u>under the sofa</u>.

2 Where (is / are) the duck?   It's / They're _____.

3 Where (is / are) the sunglasses?   It's / They're _____.

4 Where (is / are) the photo?   It's / They're _____.

4   **Listen and ✓ or ✗. Then write.**

Sally					
has got	✗	✓			
would like	✗				

Sally has got a _____ bike _____ and an _____.

She hasn't got a _____, a _____ or a _____.

She'd like a _____ and a _____. She wouldn't like a _____.

5 **Complete for yourself. Then write.**

I've got					
I'd like					

I've got _____.

I haven't got _____.

I'd like _____.

I wouldn't like _____.

6   **Can you remember? Read and answer.**

1 What colour is Grandad's hair? <u>It's grey.</u>

2 Has Rose got curly hair? _____

3 How many cousins has Charlie got? _____

4 Is Charlie wearing a green T-shirt? _____

5 Has Ola got a big nose? _____

6 Is Uncle Dan a doctor? _____

7 Does Charlie like pizza? _____

8 Can Charlie do cartwheels? _____

a | Yes, he does. | **b** | ~~It's grey.~~ | **c** | No, he isn't. |

d | No, she hasn't. | **e** | No, he can't. | **f** | Two. |

g | No, she hasn't. Her hair is straight. | **h** | No, it's blue and white. |

7 Write three questions for your friend to answer.

1 _____ ? _____

2 _____ ? _____

3 _____ ? _____

Halloween

1  **Read and match.**

1 I'm a witch. I've got six sweets.

2 I'm a monster. I've got a pumpkin.

3 I'm a ghost. I've got four sweets.

4 I'm a pumpkin. I've got a bat.

a

b

c

d

e

f

g

h

2  **Read and circle.**

1 Do you like sweets?   Yes, I do. / No, I don't.

2 Do you like bats?   Yes, I do. / No, I don't.

3 Do you like pumpkins?   Yes, I do. / No, I don't.

4 Do you like Halloween?   Yes, I do. / No, I don't.

Christmas

1 Look and write.

card	Christmas tree	present
sack	~~Santa~~	star	stocking

1 Santa   **2** _____   **3** _____   **4** _____

5 _____   **6** _____   **7** _____

2 Look and colour.

1 = red   2 = green
3 = black   4 = blue
5 = yellow

Easter

1   **Read and match.**

1 Wake up, Easter Bunny!

2 Jump, Easter Bunny!

3 Turn around, Easter Bunny!

4 Fall down, Easter Bunny!

a  **b**

c **d**

2  **Count and write.**

1 How many chicks? **5**   **2** How many flowers?

3 How many eggs?   **4** How many rabbits?

Summer fun

1 ✏️ Look and write.

| bucket | sand | sandcastle | sea | shell | ~~spade~~ |

① spade

② _____

③ _____

④ _____

⑤ _____

⑥ _____

2 ✏️✏️ Sand art! Join the dots and write.

①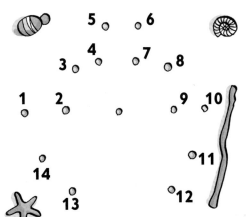

It's a _____.

②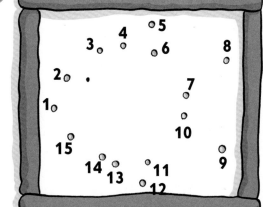

It's a _____.

1

Extra practice

1 ✏️ 😃 **Write the questions. Then say.**

① name? your What's

___What's your name?___

② are How you?

_____

③ your birthday? When's

_____

④ today? day What it is

_____

2 📖 ✏️ **Read and circle. Then write.**

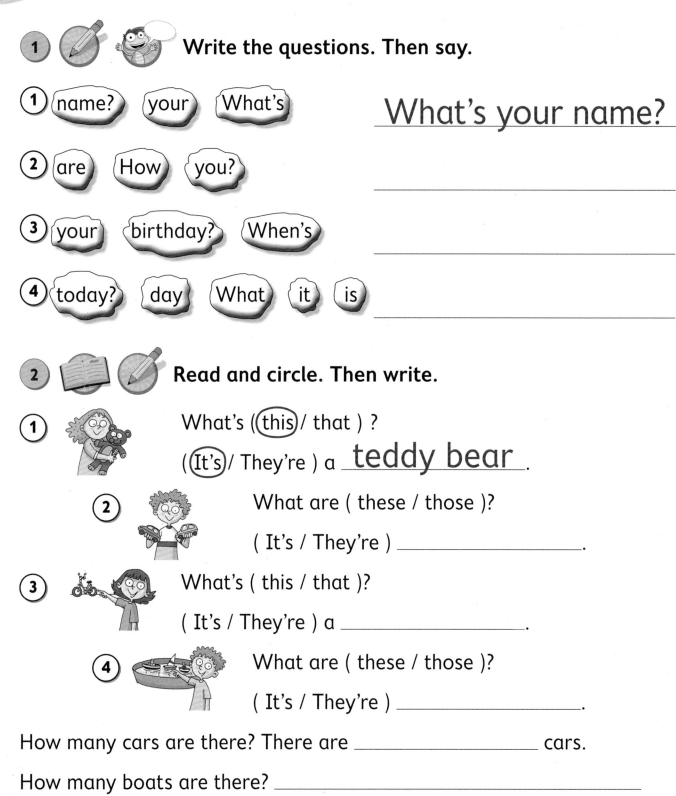

① What's (**this** / that) ?

(**It's** / They're) a ___teddy bear___.

② What are (these / those)?

(It's / They're) _____.

③ What's (this / that)?

(It's / They're) a _____.

④ What are (these / those)?

(It's / They're) _____.

How many cars are there? There are _____ cars.

How many boats are there? _____

Read and circle.

Who's ((he) / she)?   ((He's) / She's) my uncle.

Who are (they / there)?   (They're / There) my cousins.

Where's my aunt?   (He's / She's) (on / under) the sofa.

   Read and circle.

1   They're in the (living room / kitchen).

2   (There's / (There are)) two cousins.

3   The doll is (behind / on) the TV.

4   My uncle is next to my (aunt / cousin).

1 Choose and write.

can   can't   point   touch   ~~wave~~   you

1 ___Wave___ your arms.

2 _____ your fingers.

3 _____ your toes.

4 Oh, no! I _____ touch my toes.

5 Can _____ touch your toes?

6 Yes, I _____.

1 **Read and draw.**

I haven't got small eyes. I've got big eyes.

I've got a small nose and a small mouth.

I've got big ears. My hair is long and curly.

2 **Write *Yes, she has.* or *No, she hasn't.***

1 Has she got short hair?

No, she hasn't.

2 Has she got curly hair? _____

3 Has she got small eyes? _____

4 Has she got a small mouth? _____

3 **Write correct sentences.**

1 She's got a big nose. She hasn't got a big nose.
She's got a small nose.

2 She's got straight hair. _____

_____

3 She's got small ears. _____

_____

1   **Circle and write.**

It isn't (big / (small)). It's (big / small).

(It's / They're) black.

It's got _____ legs.

(It's / They're) a _____ .

(It's / They're) small.

They aren't (black / white).

They're (black / white).

They've got _____ legs.

(It's / They're) _____ .

2 **Look at Activity 1. Read and match.**

1 Are the ducks brown?

2 Is the horse big?

3 Are the ducks small?

4 Is the horse grey?

a Yes, it is.

b No, it isn't.

c No, they aren't.

d Yes, they are.

1   **Read, look and circle.**

	🐟	🍕	🍗	🍎	🍌	🍳
👦	✓	✓	✗	✓	✗	✗
👧	✗	✓	✓	✗	✓	✓

1 He ((likes) / doesn't like) fish.

2 She (likes / doesn't like) apples.

3 Does he like bananas? (Yes, he does. / No, he doesn't.)

4 Does she like chicken? (Yes, she does. / No, she doesn't.)

2   **Read and circle.**

1 There's ((some) / any) cheese.   **2** There are (some / any) apples.

3 There isn't (some / any) milk.   **4** There aren't (some / any) bananas.

3   **Look at Activity 2. Read and match.**

① Is there any cheese?   **a** No, there aren't.

② Is there any pizza?   **b** Yes, there is.

③ Are there any apples?   **c** Yes, there are.

④ Are there any beans?   **d** No, there isn't.

7

1 **Choose and write.**

am	are	I'm	like	not	purple

~~wearing~~ would

1 Are you ___**wearing**___ shoes and socks?

2 Yes, I _____.

3 _____ wearing blue shoes and pink socks.

4 _____ you wearing purple shoes?

5 No, I'm _____.

6 Would you _____ some purple shoes?

7 Yes, I _____. Thank you!

8 Now I'm wearing _____ shoes and pink socks!

1 **Choose and write.**

> do   like   mine   that   they're   those
> ~~weather~~   windy

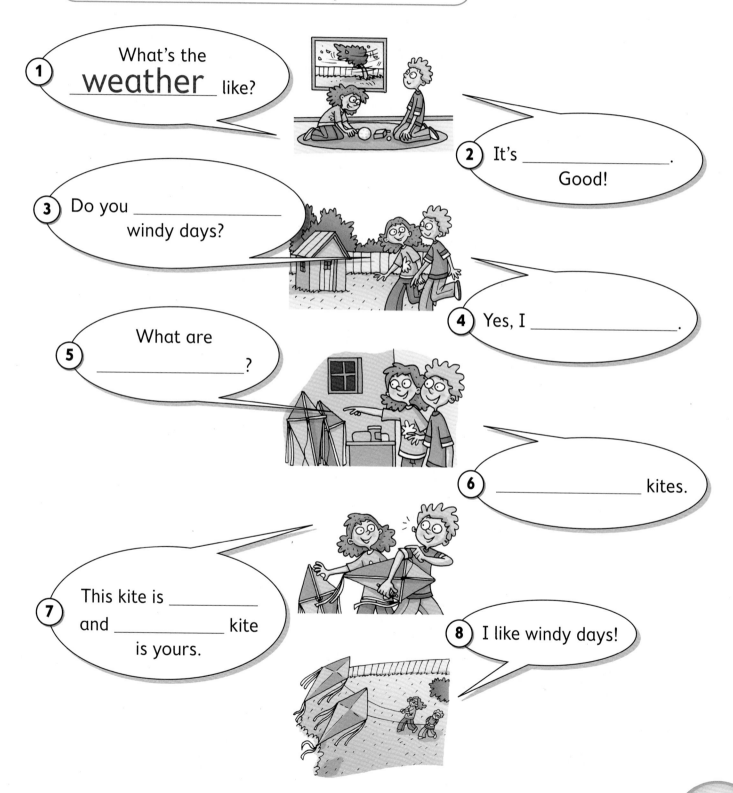

1 What's the _weather_ like?

2 It's _____.
      Good!

3 Do you _____ windy days?

4 Yes, I _____.

5 What are _____?

6 _____ kites.

7 This kite is _____ and _____ kite is yours.

8 I like windy days!

Picture dictionary

Unit 1

Toys

| train | bike | ball | car | doll | boat | teddy bear | kite | lorry |

Numbers

| 10 | 11 | 12 | 13 | 14 | 15 |
| ten | eleven | twelve | thirteen | fourteen | fifteen |

| 16 | 17 | 18 | 19 | 20 | 21 |
| sixteen | seventeen | eighteen | nineteen | twenty | twenty-one |

| 22 | 23 | 24 | 25 | 26 | 27 |
| twenty-two | twenty-three | twenty-four | twenty-five | twenty-six | twenty-seven |

| 28 | 29 | 30 | 40 | 50 |
| twenty-eight | twenty-nine | thirty | forty | fifty |

Social Science

| bus | motorbike | lorry | plane | helicopter |

Unit 2

 ## My family

daughter   son

aunt   uncle

granny   grandad

cousins

 ## At home

house

flat

hall

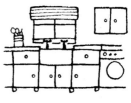

kitchen

living room

bedroom

bathroom

attic

 ## Social Science

baby

children

grandparents

young   parents   old

Unit 3

Body movements

shake your body

nod your head

wave your arms

point your fingers

touch your toes

clap your hands

stamp your feet

move your legs

 Actions

swim climb catch a ball stand on your head

throw a ball swing do cartwheels do the splits

 P.E.

pull push hop skip

Unit 4
My face

hair   ears   eyes   nose   mouth

 Adjectives

long   short   curly   straight

dark   blond   neat   messy

 Maths

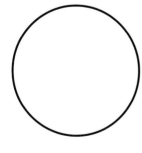 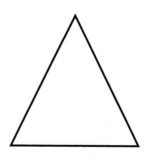  

circle   triangle   square   rectangle

Unit 5

Farm animals

horse   duck   hen   sheep   cow   goat   turkey

 ## Wild animals

bat   crow   frog   skunk

owl   lizard   rat   fox

 ## Natural Science

awake   asleep   night   day

Unit 6

Food (1)

 rice

 bananas

 pizza

 burger

 fish

 chicken

 apples

 salad

 eggs

Food (2)

 cereal

 grapes

 potatoes

 pancakes

 beans

 pineapple

 coconut

 pasta

 sweetcorn

 toast

Natural Science

 cut

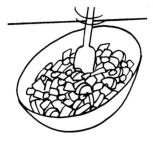 mix

 fry

 cook

Unit 7

Clothes (1)

dress

T-shirt

socks

skirt

shoes

trousers

jacket

hat

Clothes (2)

pyjamas

trainers

shirt

coat

jeans

helmet

cap

jumper

glasses

boots

Social Science

nurse

police officer

firefighter

chef

Unit 8

 Weather

windy   rainy   sunny   snowy   cloudy   stormy

 Activities

ride a bike   fly a kite   make a snowman   go for a walk

go to the beach   read a book   take a photo   watch TV

 Social Science

freezing   cold   warm   hot

Pearson Education Limited
Edinburgh Gate
Harlow
Essex CM20 2JE
England
and Associated Companies throughout the world.

Poptropica® English Islands

© Pearson Education Limited 2017

Editorial and project management by hyphen

First published 2017
Ninth impression 2019
ISBN: 978-1-2921-9823-1

Set in Fiendstar 17/21pt
Printed in Neografia, Slovakia

Acknowledgements: The publisher would like to thank Linnette Ansel Erocak, Tessa Lochowski, Laura Miller and José Luis Morales, Steve Elsworth, and Jim Rose for their contributions to this edition.

Illustrators: Chan Sui Fai, Adam Clay, Moreno Chiacchiera (Beehive Illustration), Tom Heard (The Bright Agency), Andrew Hennessey, Marek Jagucki, Sue King (Plum Pudding Illustration), Stephanine Lau, Katie McDee, Bill McGuire (Shannon Associates), Jackie Stafford, Olimpia Wong and Yam Wai Lun

Picture Credits: The publisher would like to thank the following for their kind permission to reproduce their photographs:

(Key: b-bottom; c-centre; l-left; r-right; t-top)

123RF.com: 106 (nod), 108 (hen), 109 (pizza), 109 (rice), Jacek Chabraszewski 106 (wave), Jose Manuel Gelpi Diaz 106 (point), David Franklin 110 (hat), isselee 108 (goat), nrey 108 (duck); **Alamy Stock Photo:** MIXA 106 (stamp feet); **Fotolia.com:** Robert Kneschke 35cr; **Pearson Education Ltd:** Studio 8 104 (car), 106 (move legs), Trevor Clifford 106 (clap), Rafal Trubisz 104 (doll), 106 (shake); **Shutterstock. com:** Ilya Akinshin 104 (kite), AM-STUDiO 104 (teddy bear), Blend Images 35r, Nikolay Dimitrov - ecobo 104 (train), Christopher Elwell 108 (turkey), hamurishi 104 (bike), Eric Isselee 108 (cow), 108 (horse), 108 (sheep), Karkas 110 (jacket), 110 (shoes), 110 (skirt), MShev 106 (touch toes), Maks Narodenko 109 (apples), 109 (bananas), Nattika 109 (eggs), Olga Nayashkova 109 (salad), Nitr 109 (burger), Richard Peterson 104 (ball), Olga Popova 110 (socks), pzAxe 110 (dress), sevenke 110 (T-shirt), Roman Sigaev 110 (trousers), tetxu 109 (fish), Dani Vincek 109 (chicken), Becky Wass 35l, wavebreakmedia 35cl, Mark Yuill 104 (boat)

Cover images: *Back:* **Fotolia.com:** frender r; **Shutterstock.com:** Denys Prykhodov l

All other images © Pearson Education